LISTENING FOR GOD
THROUGH
ROMANS

Lectio Divina Bible Studies

wph wesleyan publishing house
Indianapolis, Indiana

Beacon Hill Press of Kansas City
Kansas City, Missouri

Copyright © 2006 by The Wesleyan Church
Published by Wesleyan Publishing House and Beacon Hill Press of Kansas City
Indianapolis, Indiana 46250
Printed in the United States of America

ISBN-13: 978-0-89827-299-4
ISBN-10: 0-89827-299-8

Written by Keith Drury.

ABOUT THE
LECTIO DIVINA
BIBLE STUDIES

ectio divina, Latin for *divine reading,* is the ancient Christian
practice of communicating with God through the reading and
study of Scripture. Throughout history, great Christian leaders
including John Wesley have used and adapted this ancient
method of interpreting Scripture. This Bible study builds on
this practice, introducing modern readers of the Bible to the
time-honored tradition of "listening for God" through His Word.
In this series, the traditional *lectio divina* model has been revised
and expanded for use in group Bible study. Each session in this
study includes the following elements. (Latin equivalents are
noted in italics.)

- Summary   A brief overview of the session.
  Epitome

- Silence   A time of quieting oneself prior to
  Silencio   reading the Word.

- Preparation
  Praeparatio

  Focusing the mind on the central theme of the text.

- Reading
  Lectio

  Carefully reading a passage of Scripture.

- Meditation
  Meditatio

  Exploring the meaning of the Bible passage.

- Contemplation
  Contemplatio

  Yielding oneself to God's will.

- Prayer
  Oratio

  Expressing praise, thanksgiving, confession, or agreement to God.

- Incarnation
  Incarnatio

  Resolving to act on the message of Scripture.

The Lectio Divina Bible Studies invite readers to slow down, read Scripture, meditate upon it, and prayerfully respond to God's Word.

CONTENTS

Introduction	7
Relationships and Revelation	9
Nothing in My Hand I Bring	19
Choosing Our Slave Master	29
Hope in Hard Times	37
"All Who Call"—Who Can Be Saved?	45
Me: A Living and Loving Sacrifice	53
The Debt I Owe	61
Judging Disputable Matters	71

INTRODUCTION

For many Christians, an introduction to Romans comes early in their faith journeys. Evangelists frequently use key verses from this letter to lead converts to salvation. For example, in 3:23, we see that no one is exempt from the sin problem. In 6:23 we see that the punishment for sin is always death, but that through the death of Jesus, God offers the free gift of a new way—life that lasts forever. And in 10:9–10, we see that the way to receive this gift is by confessing belief in Jesus Christ and especially in the fact that God resurrected Him—proving His deity and His ultimate power over death.

But the letter is richer yet for the seasoned believer. The believer who may be beleaguered by opposition, who may feel distant from God due to circumstances, who may be worn down by the battle. Who can forget the energizing words of Romans

8:38–39: "For I am convinced that neither death nor life, neither angels nor demons, neither the present nor the future, nor any powers, neither height nor depth, nor anything else in all creation, will be able to separate us from the love of God that is in Christ Jesus our Lord"?

Paul wrote this letter to a church he'd never visited. He longed to meet these believers in person, but at this stage in his third missionary journey (described in Acts 15–21), the severe opposition he was meeting among the Jews, particularly in Jerusalem, made him unsure that he'd ever reach Rome. So, he wrote this letter that so beautifully describes the universal truth of salvation by faith for Jews and Gentiles together.

It is a reasoned, intelligent argument of the whole message of the gospel. A favorite of believers down through the centuries, including Martin Luther who called it "the very purest Gospel," this letter to the Romans is worthy of study and appreciation by all who seek the salvation and comfort of God.

RELATIONSHIPS AND REVELATION

Listening for God through Romans 1:8–25

SUMMARY

Even before creation, there were relationships—between God the Father, Son, and Holy Spirit. The Trinity loves and communes with each other. God, by His very nature, is relational. Then we came on the scene. God created and relates to us. And He inspires love between His children. Paul loved the Roman church and longed to be with them. Today's church is a loving community of relationships that reflects (in its best moments) the love among the Godhead. The church is relational, in the image of God.

But how can we relate to God if we don't know Him? We can only know Him because He has made himself known. He revealed himself through "natural revelation"—in nature and in human conscience. No person born on earth can say, "I never heard." We have no excuse, since we all are witnesses of God through nature. The blowing wind. A newborn baby's cry. A field of flowers in full bloom.

But nature isn't even the best picture of God ever taken. Jesus Christ is—He is Revelation with a capital "R," *the* Revelation of God. In Jesus Christ we meet *very God*. When we enter a relationship with Christ, we enter a relationship with the Godhead and with the family of God, for none can call God, Father, who does not call the church brother and sister.

SILENCE ✝ LISTEN FOR GOD

Quietly imagine the interplay of communication, love, and fellowship between the Father, Son, and Holy Spirit *before* creation. Imagine what they might have said to each other as an example of an ideal relationship.

PREPARATION ✝ FOCUS YOUR THOUGHTS

What person do you long to see who is far away?

What group of people whom you've never met would you like to visit?

Tell about a time when you felt closer to God when in nature.

READING ✝ HEAR THE WORD

When we read Romans, we are "looking over the shoulders" of the first-century, conservative Jewish Christians who received the letter. It is perhaps the most orderly attempt in the New Testament at answering the questions conservative, deep-thinking Christian Jews would have about the gospel. The way of salvation to the Jew had been clear. They would think: *We are God's chosen people; the law was given to us; we attempt to obey the law; sacrifices and rituals provide atonement for our sins where we miss the mark; and righteousness comes by obedience to God's commands.*

Paul preached a different kind of gospel: a righteousness that came through faith by grace due to Christ's own once-for-all sacrifice. It is no wonder conservative, well-behaved Jewish Christians resisted Paul's new, seemingly "liberal" teaching. Would people "saved by faith and not obedience" then discard any commitment to holy living? Did Paul's teaching promote libertinism—a doctrine allowing for promiscuous living since "works don't matter"? Was the law useless? Why did God give the law if He was going to do this bait-and-switch scheme later on, making the law invalid? And, was being the "chosen people" wasted? Does the coming of Christ destroy the Old Testament?

Romans 1 is the preface to this wonderful book—perhaps the greatest attempt by Paul to explain the gospel in a way that satisfies the human mind. Read this first section of Romans as if you were opening a letter from the famed and loved Apostle Paul—read it as a letter.

MEDITATION ✢ ENGAGE THE WORD

Meditate on Romans 1:8–17

What are some of the verbs Paul uses to express his relationship with the Roman church in this passage? What do they tell us about Paul's relationship with these people?

Describe Paul's relationship with the Romans. Though Paul had not yet visited the Roman church he apparently already knew many in the church. Glance over his farewell in Romans 15:1–16 to find hints describing the sort of people who got the letter of Romans.

What was the Roman church "famous" for across the then-known world? While our intention should never be fame, what sort of things today could get a church a reputation for famous faith?

Paul claimed to serve God with his "whole heart" — a heart fully devoted to following Jesus Christ. Yet we know there are plenty of half-hearted Christians. How can a half-hearted Christian become whole-hearted?

The Roman Christians were already believers, yet Paul longs to preach the gospel to them that is "the power of God unto salvation." Today we think of preaching the gospel as something to do for unbelievers. What value is it for *believers* to hear the gospel?

What about the gospel message might tempt a Christian (or preacher like Paul) to be "ashamed" or embarrassed by it? Can you tell of a time when you were embarrassed to proclaim the gospel?

What is the difference between righteousness *in fact* and righteousness *in faith*? A Christian's position can be "perfect in Christ," yet our performance (daily life) may still fall short. How does God raise our performance up to our position?

Reflect on the sidebar quote by Anthony J. D'Angelo, then ask how it might appear to others that we value possessions more than relationships. What practical actions can we take to reverse this impression?

> Treasure your relationships, not your possessions.
> —Anthony J. D'Angelo

Meditate on Romans 1:18–20

We don't like to talk about the "wrath of God," but Paul saw God's wrath already being revealed. Using the context of these verses asks if God reveals His wrath today. To whom does He do this and why?

Ponder the sidebar quote on God's wrath by Joseph Ratzinger. Close your eyes and visualize this picture in your mind—a raging river into which people determine to walk. How would seeing God's wrath this way change our views?

> The wrath of God is a way of saying that I have been living in a way that is contrary to the love that is God. Anyone who begins to live and grow away from God, who lives away from what is good, is turning his life toward wrath.
> —Joseph Ratzinger

The clearest revelation of God is in Jesus Christ, of course, not nature. But God has already revealed Himself in creation making all humans accountable for the revelation they have received. What does nature tell us about God?

Paul argues that all humans are accountable due to this "natural revelation," so they have no excuses when they face the judgment. Rather than taking a side trip into discussing those who have never heard, think about yourself—what have *you* heard that makes you more accountable than those who have only natural revelation?

Meditate on the quote by William Cowper. How does nature fall short of telling us the full story of God? What does Jesus Christ reveal about God that is far more complete than the revelation of nature?

> Nature is a good name for an effect whose cause is God.
>
> —William Cowper

Meditate on Romans 1:21–25

How might a person know God yet not glorify Him? How did the idolaters of this passage know God?

How bad must it get before God gives people over to their own sinfulness, in a sense letting them go to the logical end of their path? This passage seems to be more about a people than a person. Does God abandon nations? Tribes? Denominations? Local churches? Can you think of any time in biblical history where God seemed to withdraw from a people and let them continue on their sinful path—at least for a time?

CONTEMPLATION ✝ REFLECT AND YIELD

If God has best revealed himself in Jesus, what should you do to know more about what Jesus Christ was like?

Oratio PRAYER ✝ RESPOND TO GOD

In group sentence prayers, first *praise* God for the beauty of creation, then *thank* Him for Jesus Christ's revelation, and finally *ask* Him to help your church illustrate loving relationships.

Incarnatio INCARNATION ✝ LIVE THE WORD

How will your schedule change when you follow up on your commitment to know Christ better?

How will you live out your purpose to both know God and glorify Him in the coming week?

NOTHING IN MY HAND I BRING

Listening for God through Romans 3:9–31

SUMMARY

In Romans 1 as Paul is delineating the nasty sins of the Gentiles, you can imagine his Jewish readers nodding their heads with condemning amens. But in the next chapter he springs a trap on the Jews by reminding them that they, too, are sinners, and thus they, too, have no excuse. Paul does begin chapter 3 by admitting some advantages to being a Jew (they had Scripture, etc.), but ultimately there is none righteous—not one, because all have sinned, both Jew and Gentile.

Paul paints the Jews into the same corner with the Gentiles: sinners desperately in need of God's grace. He writes Romans to announce a new way to be righteous. Keeping the law perfectly was one way, but nobody could do it perfectly. This new path to righteousness is through faith in Christ. If our righteousness comes from God through Christ alone, we have nothing to boast about but Jesus Christ and God's mercy.

SILENCE ✝ LISTEN FOR GOD

Quiet your heart by slowly repeating the following three words— taste them as you repeat them—*love, grace, faith.*

PREPARATION ✝ FOCUS YOUR THOUGHTS

Tell about a time when you had absolutely no hope to solve a problem with your own resources—you were completely help-less and had to trust someone else to pull you through. Tell of another time when you tried to fix something on your own but only made it worse.

Lectio READING ✞ HEAR THE WORD

After outlining the absolute hopelessness of the Gentiles to be righteous (in chapter 1), Paul then includes the Jews (in chapter 2)—for they were just as hopelessly unable to perfectly keep the Jewish law. So both Gentiles and Jews are in the same boat: sinking in hopeless and inadequate self-righteousness. The obvious response from the conservative Jewish Christians was, "then what advantage has there been in being a Jew at all?" In chapter 3 Paul responds to that question. The Jews had the law. They had Scriptures. They understood sin and holiness. But ultimately what good did it do them, since they couldn't live up to the expectations?

When Paul quotes the Old Testament to prove the universality of unrighteousness, he quotes it from memory—thus he sometimes paraphrases the original words. This common rabbinic method of stringing together a series of quotes from Scripture to make a point is called a *charaz*—literally "stringing pearls."

Christians sometimes wrongly believe that the Old Testament God was a nationalistic civil God of the Jewish nation, and Jesus came to present a God of all people. This is not so. The Old Testament Jews considered "the God of the Jews" to be the One True God of all the world, and even when they "accepted" gods of other nations as existing, they claimed these gods were demigods at best under the overall command of *the* God—Yahweh, the Lord of hosts.

Read the entire section of Scripture aloud with forcefulness, as if you are a lawyer making a case before a jury.

MEDITATION ✝ ENGAGE THE WORD

Meditate on Romans 3:9–20

What were the advantages the Jews had over the Gentiles before Jesus came? What advantages do people raised in the church have today? Yet, even though some groups start off with some seeming advantages, in what ways are we all absolutely equal?

Paul strung together like pearls at least five Psalms and a verse from Isaiah in his poetic description of human nature gone sour without Christ. Which of these are matters of character? Behavior? Tongue?

Think about what you would be like without any presence of Christ in your life.

The Jews cherished the commandments and the Law hoping they might become righteous by keeping all the rules. Paul blasts this hope in the concluding verse of this section by citing the real purpose of the commandments and law. What does he describe as the *real* purpose of the Law?

Reflect on the quote by Lesslie Newbigin suggesting the essence of sin is assuming we can achieve righteousness on our own. What can ordinary Christians do to remind themselves and each other of this important truth of Romans? What could be the dangers of excessive emphasis on this truth?

> If there were a righteousness which a man could have of his own, then we should have to concern ourselves with the question of how it can be imparted to him. But there is not. The idea of a righteousness of one's own is the quintessence of sin.
>
> —Lesslie Newbigin

Meditate on Romans 3:21–26

Paul describes two ways to be righteous: *Keeping all the rules* or *trusting Christ by faith*. The first focuses on what we can do for ourselves, the second on what God can do for us (and has already done). The first route is hopeless, but the second has been revealed in Jesus Christ. What is the difference between keeping rules and trusting rule-keeping?

Ponder the C. S. Lewis quote. What is a "spuriously good conscience"? How can good people more easily trust their goodness to count for something? What sort of things might we say to ourselves that displace Christ as our only hope? Rules often focus

> Nothing gives one a more spuriously good conscience than keeping rules, even if there has been a total absence of all real charity and faith.
>
> –C.S. Lewis

on the "don'ts" of Christian living rather than the do's. If we were to have more rules for the do's, what might they be?

Paul argues that God was demonstrating His justice by providing Jesus Christ as a means to righteousness. What? Wouldn't God's justice have merely condemned men for their sin? Either explain or meditate on what J. A. Bengel calls the "supreme paradox of the gospel."

Meditate on Romans 3:27–31

Since God has thrown the trust-Christ rope to us, we who are drowning in our attempts to be good enough for God should have nothing left to boast about. How do we appear to boast of our goodness to others, to God, or even privately to ourselves?

Think about Paul's whole argument here—being righteous by grace through faith alone and not through our own goodness. What would seem to be the logical answer to this question: So then we don't have to keep the law right? What was Paul's answer to this? Why?

Think about the verse from the Charles Wesley hymn, "O for a Thousand Tongues." We're familiar with individuals casting their hope on Christ for righteousness, but can a *nation* do this? If a nation (or a church or any other group of people) were to trust Christ for righteousness (not just to help them win wars, but truly trust Christ for righteousness) how would a *group* do this?

> Look unto him, ye nations, own Your God, ye fallen race; Look, and be saved through faith alone, Be justified by grace. See all your sins on Jesus laid: The Lamb of God was slain, His soul was once an offering made For every soul of man.
>
> —Charles Wesley
> ("O for a Thousand Tongues")

CONTEMPLATION ✝ REFLECT AND YIELD

Think about how you can submit to the gospel that grants right-eousness by faith and not by your own performance. Take some action of submission to it by journaling your surrender to this great plan of salvation.

PRAYER ✝ RESPOND TO GOD

Perhaps the best response in prayer is to thank God for His unmerited favor—grace to us though we are undeserving. Pray around the circle in this vein, even if it is repetitive.

INCARNATION ✝ LIVE THE WORD

Make a list of everything you could offer as evidence that you are a good person, then bury the list in your church yard or your own backyard in a place you will pass by often. Whenever you pass that spot, recall the true source of righteousness.

Make a motto or plaque reading, "Nothing in my hand I bring; simply to thy cross I cling."

CHOOSING OUR SLAVE MASTER

Listening for God through Romans 6:11–23; 7:14–24

SUMMARY

P aul argued that all have sinned. The Jews were caretakers of the Law, but it didn't really help them be righteous, for nobody can keep it perfectly. Jews and Gentiles alike are under condemnation. The Jewish Law didn't help them get off the hook.

Jesus brought with Him a new way to be righteous—by faith, not by keeping the Law. So, does that mean we can sin boldly since we are saved by faith alone? "By no means" is Paul's answer. We were once slaves to sin, but now we are freed from sin and are slaves to Christ. Paul leaves us no in-between position: we are either slaves to sin or slaves to Christ. We can't serve both masters. If we are slaves to sin, we can't be good even if we want to. And if we are slaves to Christ, we can't keep on sinning. It is slavery either way: to sin or to Christ. Our choice is which master to serve.

SILENCE ✟ LISTEN FOR GOD

To prepare your heart to hear God speak, silently ponder the following mystery: "Slavery is freedom."

PREPARATION ✟ FOCUS YOUR THOUGHTS

Discuss how each of the following groups of people can be free, and yet not free: Children. College students. Single adults. Young married couples without children. Divorced adults. Empty nesters. Aged nursing home residents.

Imagine what a person would be like who was absolutely and totally free.

READING ✟ HEAR THE WORD

Before reading, capture the flow of the context. Paul's point so far: 1) No one is righteous (neither Jew nor Gentile) since all have sinned and need grace. 2) Jesus brought a new way to be righteous—by faith through God's grace. 3) Abraham himself was even justified by faith (chapter 4) by trusting God's promise (which was credited to him as righteousness). 4) God demonstrated His love for us when Christ died at just the right time. 5) Sin entered the world through Adam, but life and righteousness entered through Jesus Christ, the new Adam; and 6) What Adam ruined, Christ restores.

The question behind chapter six is if we're saved by grace through faith and not works, why not keep on sinning? Paul's answer: By no means! We are either slaves to sin or Christ. If we serve Christ, we can't keep on sinning. The law is like a dead spouse: we are free. Taking on the part of an unbeliever, Paul describes a person in slavery to sin who can't do the good he knows is right and can't avoid the sin he knows is wrong. Chapter 8 is the hopeful glorious end to the matter, but we cover that in the next lesson.

Have two people read these sections of Scripture—the first read the selection from chapter 6 with a reasoned, logical voice, the second read the selection from chapter 7 with emotion and deep feeling.

MEDITATION ✝ ENGAGE THE WORD

Meditate on Romans 6:11–14

To Paul what would a Christian do to "let sin reign" in her life? Ponder the "do not's" or "shall not's" in this passage, then describe what sort of lifestyle a Christian is supposed to have related to sin and sinning.

Paul will later address offering our bodies to God (12:1–2), but here he plants the idea of "offering parts of your body to sin." Name some body parts and the corresponding sins they can be offered to. Now rename those parts, explaining how they could be offered to God.

What does it mean that "sin shall not be your master"? How much sinning can a Christian commit before being mastered by sin? What percentage of people today

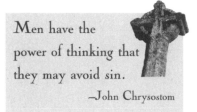

Men have the power of thinking that they may avoid sin.

—John Chrysostom

would agree with John Chrysostom's quote?

Meditate on Romans 6:15–23

Paul was accused of preaching that salvation by faith meant Christians could live any way they wanted, and Paul's church in Corinth gave some credence to that accusation. Paul defends his gospel against that charge. Find and read the phrases where he rejects the charge that he is preaching a "sinning religion."

Paul alludes to the past sins these Roman Christians were now ashamed of. What are some of the shameful, now-abandoned sins you know have been committed by people who are now saved?

(Be careful to not name names, but just remind the group of the shameful deeds once done by people who now serve Christ.)

Find and repeat all the phrases in this passage that are past tense: *were, used to, have been*, etc. Then find and repeat all the phrases that are present tense: *are, now, have become*, etc. From this exercise what picture emerges of Christian life related

> Think, and be careful what thou art within; For there is sin in the desire of sin; Think, and be thankful, in a different case; For there is grace in the desire of grace.
> —Ralph Waldo Emerson

to sinning? What is the meaning of the Ralph Waldo Emerson quote on sin and grace?

In Romans 6:23 Paul's climaxing discussion of the relationship of sin and human beings points toward the destination of the two slaveries. What meaning do you get from this verse in context that expands your traditional understanding of it?

Meditate on Romans 7:14–24

This passage may be the most misunderstood passage of Scripture. Paul employs a rhetorical device here when using the first person "I," as a parent might do when preparing a high school senior for college, "Okay, the alarm goes off again, but I've stayed up late so I hit the snooze button and forget going to classes; soon I'm flunking out." Paul here describes the life of the slave of sin using first-person rhetoric. Read the section slowly, phrase by phrase, with this thought in mind: to better understand his role as a pre-Christian sinner.

Despite Paul's obvious original meaning above, many Christians through history (including many in the holiness movement) have taken this passage to describe an in-between state of a Christian—a person saved but not yet entirely sanctified. Without getting into a heated argument over it, revisit the passage and make the argument both ways.

Using the Bill Maher quote, think about the relationship of sin and disease.

> Everything that used to be a sin is now a disease.
>
> —Bill Maher

Finally, consider a more important issue about the Bible. First, think of examples where Christians today use a Bible verse to mean something it never meant originally when it was written— what some call the "near and far meanings." What do you think? Can we get meanings from the Bible that the original author never intended? Does God ever mean something in Scripture that the original writer and readers never understood? If not, how do we know for sure what the original meaning of the author was? If so, how do we guard against going off the deep end and making the Bible mean whatever we want it to mean?

CONTEMPLATION ✟ REFLECT AND YIELD

While a Christian is not a slave to sin but to Christ, in what ways are some parts of your body being tempted to return to slavery to sin? Consider your ears, mouth, and mind for starters.

PRAYER ✟ RESPOND TO GOD

Pray sentence-prayers of gratitude and praise for being freed from slavery to sin. Be bold in affirming your servanthood to Christ and not to sin.

INCARNATION ✝ LIVE THE WORD

Write on a tiny card in secret code or symbol the part of your body you will offer as a living sacrifice to God every moment this week. Put the card somewhere where you will see it often.

HOPE IN
HARD TIMES

Listening for God through Romans 8:18-39

SUMMARY

P aul was suffering and had experienced suffering all through his ministry. So were the Roman Christians. They faced opposition and persecution for their faith. Here in this chapter Paul puts his and their present sufferings into perspective — in the light of future glory and hope. Compared to what we will experience in the future and what Christ experienced in the past, our present sufferings don't even make it on the comparison graph.

Paul sets out what will become the song of thousands of future Christians who face suffering — he encourages them and us to become "more than conquerors" in trials and tribulations. We may be stripped of position, authority, possessions, and life itself, but we Christians will be rich anyway: Christ died for us. We

have the Spirit within helping us pray. Christ is in heaven interceding for us; and nothing in heaven, on earth, or even under the
earth can separate us from God's love. Face it: if God is for us,
who can be against us?

SILENCE ✝ LISTEN FOR GOD

Open your Bible, and with closed eyes lay your hands on Romans
8 spending a full three minutes symbolically preparing to sense
God speak through His Word today.

PREPARATION ✝ FOCUS YOUR THOUGHTS

The labor-birth sequence is a wonderful example of perspective—
given the glory of a new birth, the pains of the moment melt away.
What other example of gain-after-pain can you think of?

READING ✝ HEAR THE WORD

In the preceding chapter Paul sets up the argument by describing a
person in bondage to the law of sin and death—unable to do what
he knows is right and to resist doing what he knows as wrong. It is
a description of wretched slavery to sin that ends with a cry for
deliverance: "Who will deliver me from this body of death?" The
answer is Jesus Christ, and chapter 8 describes the rescue in such

glorious terms it is hard to read it without responding by singing grateful praise to God. We are free of the law of sin and can obey Christ because we are controlled by the Spirit. Thus we put to death the deeds of sin as children of God, and we prepare for future glory where even our bodies will be redeemed. When we pray, the Spirit helps us pray. With all this in mind we can face anything—with God for us who can be against us? Nothing can separate us from God's love.

Arrange for someone to practice reading the entire chapter of Romans 8 as a dramatic reading. Don't follow along in your Bible in a studious manner, but rather listen to the Word the way it was heard in the first century—by hearing it read to an entire church gathered. It will be almost impossible not to feel blessed by these glorious words.

MEDITATION ✝ ENGAGE THE WORD

Meditate on Romans 8:18–27

Paul (and later Augustine) observes that "the fall" corrupted both human beings and the creation itself. Since humanity is fallen, how much do we "let it be" and live with the fallenness of humans? How much do we resist it? How would creation—the environment—be different if there had been no fall? When will humans and creation be finally and totally liberated from the fall? In the mean time, how much should Christians try to help God reverse the effects of the fall in their own lives? In creation?

Paul presents both creation and humans as "groaning" for deliverance from the fall. Yet as we groan, we have hope for future deliverance, because we have a deposit or the first fruits of the Holy Spirit. How does a person know he has the Holy Spirit? What evidence is there? If hope is the antidote to impatience, what attitudes are at the root of impatience?

Not only does creation groan for deliverance from the fall (as we join in), but the Holy Spirit groans too—interceding for us "with groans that words cannot express." Tell about some past feelings you have had that words could not express, times when "unintelligible groaning" (out loud or under your breath) was the best way to convey the emotion. About what, do you feel so deeply *spiritually* that when you try to express it, your feelings are closer to groans than words?

Read church father Augustine's quote on Christ's suffering. With eyes closed repeat what Jesus might have thought or said during His suffering—both what

> God had one Son on earth without sin, but never one without suffering.
>
> —St. Augustine

He actually said and what He could have thought. Say these words aloud around the circle. Then ponder in silence Christ's sufferings (don't *discuss* them—*ponder* them). Let meaning come to you from God. Then open your eyes, and share the meaning you got from this meditation on Christ's suffering.

Meditate on Romans 8:28–30

How would the Romans have applied the idea that God works in all things for good? What did God want us to get? How does this approach play out in a worldview? How does it apply to earthquakes and hurricanes? To cancer? Apply it to the suffering the Roman Christians and Paul were experiencing. When does it "work out for good"?

Read Jim Watkins' quote on the context and the why of Romans 8:28. Discuss how "all things" can be worked toward the end of conforming us to be more like Christ. What are some of the uses of this verse that fall short of its deeper meaning?

> I had never noticed the verse that followed Romans 8:28 . . . Yep, I had missed the whole "purpose" of Romans 8:28: "To be conformed to the likeness of his Son . . ."
>
> —Jim Watkins

Meditate on the verbs of "God's Great Arrangement" for the church (verses 29–30): *foreknew, predestined, conformed, called, justified, glorified.* If this does not mean "God picked who would be saved and who would be lost and there's nothing you can do about it," then how else would you explain it?

Meditate on *Romans* 8:31–39

What are some charges that might have been brought against the Romans? Paul? Yourself? How does Jesus Christ intercede for us differently than the Holy Spirit's intercession a few verses before? Which passages in Hebrews does this bring to mind?

When we are suffering, we tend to think God doesn't love us. Without parsing the meaning too deeply, simply repeat aloud, together seven times, the last two verses in this section on the love of God. Then sing together whatever songs come to mind.

> The love of God is
> greater far
> Than tongue or pen
> can ever tell;
> It goes beyond the highest star,
> And reaches to the lowest hell;
> —Frederick M. Lehman

Bypass your mind for the moment, and let your heart hear these words of God in Scripture and song. What did God say to you just now?

CONTEMPLATION ✝ REFLECT AND YIELD

God's word calls for submission—what truth has He given you that you choose to submit to from this Scripture?

PRAYER ✝ RESPOND TO GOD

Sit in attentive silence to hear God's direct word to you on suffering, hope, and His love. When you hear it, speak it aloud in first person—in the tense God would use in speaking to you.

INCARNATION ✝ LIVE THE WORD

How will you think differently about suffering and difficulty starting this week? How will you think differently about God's love?

"ALL WHO CALL"—
WHO CAN BE SAVED

Listening for God through Romans 10:1–15

SUMMARY

The book of Romans is an elaborate, logical argument describing how salvation by faith applies to the Jews and Gentiles alike. Paul's argument is made to Jews and includes some startling points. Chapter 9 is an example of this. Paul has just argued that a sovereign God could do anything He wants— harden Pharaoh's heart or make of clay vessels for any purpose, noble or ignoble. Since God can do whatever He wants, who are the Jews to say He can't invite Gentiles on the basis of faith?

In the chapter before us, Paul continues the argument that both Jews and Gentiles are saved by faith. It is easy to see the Jews as stubborn in their refusal to receive this easier way to righteousness.

But are we much better? Do we really believe our salvation is by faith alone? *Really?*

SILENCE ✝ LISTEN FOR GOD

Slowly repeat at least ten times, person-by-person, around the circle, "On Christ the solid rock I stand."

PREPARATION ✝ FOCUS YOUR THOUGHTS

Though we easily affirm the idea of "salvation is by faith through grace alone," what do we often tend to add under our breath as the small print when considering another person's salvation?

READING ✝ HEAR THE WORD

There are two kinds of Jews to consider when reading Romans. First are the *Jewish Christians*. These were converted Jews who followed Christ and were in the church at Rome. They were likely the "conservative wing" of the church, hoping for holy living and greater emphasis on devotion and piety. These conservative Christian Jews may have continued keeping their life-long convictions carried over from Judaism, including refusal to eat meat that had been sacrificed to idols and careful observance of the Sabbath. They held a reverence for the Law and did not want to see it flicked away as irrelevant.

While they had faith in Christ, they may have been worried that too much emphasis on grace and faith might open the door to all kinds of sinful living in the church. Thus they were cautious about Paul's teaching and its effect, though they were not obstinate.

However there is a second group of Jews — the *Israelites*. These were the Jews through history and in Paul's time who refused to believe. While Paul intertwines these two groups throughout Romans, it is predominantly this second group he addresses in this section of Romans.

Read the section twice today, verse-by-verse, around the circle — the first time for practice and the second time as a formal reading.

MEDITATION ✝ ENGAGE THE WORD

Meditate on Romans 10:1–4

Paul's heart's desire and prayer focused on the Israelites' salvation. What person do you focus on for salvation? What *group* of people?

What was the knowledge the Jews lacked accompanying their passion? Without using names, describe someone zealous who lacks adequate knowledge. Again, without using names, describe someone knowledgeable who is passionless. Name a person you think is a good example of a balanced, "knowledgeable yet zealous" Christian.

Discuss Colorado preacher John Swanger's quote describing the dangers of stagnancy or hysteria. Which of these two are you personally more inclined toward— knowledge or passion? Which side

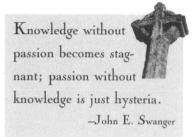

Knowledge without passion becomes stagnant; passion without knowledge is just hysteria.
    —John E. Swanger

does your church tilt toward? What can a church do to correct an imbalance one way or the other? What can a person do?

Paul accused the Jews of trying to establish their own righteousness rather than receiving righteousness from God. How can we today tend toward this error? How is getting your righteousness from God a matter of submission? What are the potential dangers of this truth?

Meditate on Romans 10:5–13

Paul alludes to the *nearness* of salvation, reminding us we do not have to go up to heaven nor travel down to death to fetch its meaning. What other Scriptures does God bring to mind that also remind us we needn't go to extravagant means to find salvation or truth? Tell about some of the extravagant lengths to which people have gone in the past to find righteousness.

Think about Beatrice Breck's quote about obedience and love. Relate it to parenting. How does a parent inspire love that prompts obedience? As for ourselves, what are signs that a person or church is entering through the obedience doorway instead of the love entrance?

> As for obedience and love, the mistake the Jews made (and many Christians as well) was to try to get to love through the door of obedience rather than entering into obedience through the doorway of love. Loving God leads to keeping His commandments, not the reverse.
>
> –Beatrice Breck

Read Acts 17:27, and ponder Paul's comment in Athens. Now ponder the nearness of God. Is God near to *everybody* or only some? Is He near to people who have never heard? Is God already near to unbelieving people we work with and live beside? If so, how would this affect our approach to them?

What are the "two spiritual laws" in this section—what two things must one do to be saved? Meditate on the terms *confess* and *believe*, then visualize the following four words in a four-way diagram in your mind—*believe, heart, confess, mouth*. What does God say to you through this diagram?

How long can a person believe in her heart without confessing with her mouth? Turn to John 19:38 for more clarity. Then discuss Beau Hummel's quote. Tell about anyone you know who was a secret disciple for a while.

> *S*ecret discipleship is only a temporary condition; sooner or later the secrecy will destroy the discipleship or the discipleship will destroy the secrecy.
>
> —Beau Hummel

Find, then meditate on, these three words in this section: *anyone, all, everyone*. What hymns or choruses do they remind you of? What other Scriptures? What insights does God give you through these words in their context?

Paul here makes the astonishing claim, "There is no difference between Jew and Gentile." Today we might say, "Duh!" for it is obvious to us. Imagine yourself a Jew in that day receiving this truth. How might you have responded? What other barriers between peoples did Paul melt down elsewhere? Can you find those Scriptures?

Meditate on Romans 10:14–15

Organize in forward sequence the five "salvation process verbs" in verse 14 (*call, believe, hear, preaching, sent*). Meditate on each word, listening for God's thoughts. Share them with your group. Try to tell your own salvation story using this five-point outline.

CONTEMPLATION † REFLECT AND YIELD

Articulate what God is saying to you personally today through these Scriptures. Offer what He *may* be saying to your church or group.

PRAYER ✝ RESPOND TO GOD

Of all the verses studied, which phrases does God bring back to your mind now as you quietly spend moments in attentive prayer?

INCARNATION ✝ LIVE THE WORD

What single action could you take to begin responding to today's Scripture? When will you take it? Who will hold you accountable?

ME: A LIVING AND LOVING SACRIFICE

Listening for God through Romans 12:1–21

SUMMARY

H aving systematically laid out his theoretical argument in the first eleven chapters, Paul turns now to application: how to live in the real world in light of these truths. He has argued that the wicked Gentiles are under God's wrath but the Jews are no better off without Christ—all have sinned and thus faith is the only way to be justified. While death and slavery to sin comes through Adam; life, freedom, and victory over sin come through faith in Christ.

Now in Romans 12 we start to see how these heady doctrines play out in daily life, starting with presenting ourselves as living sacrifices of love—not just to God, but for others, as well.

SILENCE ✝ LISTEN FOR GOD

Ponder this phrase as a means of slowing down and focusing:
Given who God is and what He's done . . . how shall we then live?

PREPARATION ✝ FOCUS YOUR THOUGHTS

How might we treat other people differently if we *knew* there was
no God? Compare theses approaches: a) treat others the way they
deserve to be treated; b) treat others in light of how God has
treated us.

READING ✝ HEAR THE WORD

The body and body parts are an important idea in Romans. In
the world at that time, Greek thinking considered the body to be
evil and only the spirit of a person good. It was widely thought
in the secular world of Paul's day that a person could never be
free of sin until he was free of his body. But the spirit was a
different matter. The spirit could be good and clean and beauti-
ful. Thus one can readily see how people in those days might
actually come up with a religion where their bodies sinned

because that's what human bodies do, while their spirits remained holy and pure inside them. Paul rejected this idea completely (as did all Christian thinking). To the early Christians the body was good and God-given, and it could be sanctified along with the spirit.

In the ancient world it was common for worshippers to offer body parts to their god. These are called votives, and there are thousands of these fired-clay body parts that have been excavated at various altars of ancient gods: an ear, a hand, eye, and many private parts. The original readers would have had this common practice in mind when reading Romans 12. However Paul calls us to make a living sacrifice—not clay votives, but our whole body to God. He reminds us that we then become a body part of the body of Christ, each with his or her own role and place of service.

Arrange for someone to practice ahead of time a staccato reading of this chapter. Without anyone following along, have the reader move rapidly through the passage piling one instruction on another, so quickly that nobody can ponder one individual instruction so much as capture the whole effect of the described lifestyle of a Christian. Read in such a way that everyone sees the whole picture, not the individual details.

MEDITATION ✝ ENGAGE THE WORD

Meditate on Romans 12:1–2

What sort of mercy has God shown to humans that deserves our responding with sacrifice?

How has Paul been speaking of the *body* so far in Romans? In light of this, what are we to do with our bodies? What truths emerge as you meditate on the phrase "living sacrifice"? Imagine a mental video of yourself offering an Old Testament sacrifice as a Jew. Now visualize yourself offering this living sacrifice. Close your eyes, and share aloud what you see in your mind.

Besides no longer conforming to the Jewish sacrificial system, we are also urged not to conform to the world's pattern. What are some patterns that make up the world's system?

God alone transforms our minds so we can think differently, but He uses ordinary channels. What are the ordinary means of grace God most often uses to make a worldly person think Christianly? How is God's will (as detailed in the rest of the chapter) different than how we often think of God's will?

Read the William Barclay quote, then ponder and discuss: If our living sacrifice treatment of others would be fully modeled after Jesus' example, *how far would we be willing to go*? How can we get this kind of love?

> Love always involves responsibility, and love always involves sacrifice. And we do not really love Christ unless we are prepared to face His task and to take up His Cross.
>
> —William Barclay

Meditate on Romans 12:3–8

Some Roman Christians apparently thought they were better than other Christians. (We will see why in chapter 14.) Why are we urged to avoid this brand of thinking? What could make a Christian think he is better than others today?

Paul claims that as a part of the body of Christ "each member belongs to all the others." Using the incomplete list of gifts in this section, describe how each gift belongs to the body more than the individual. How would these gifts play out if seen as possessed by the church instead of as "*my* spiritual gift."

Read Paul's quote from 1 Corinthians 12, then do this humorous exercise: For each of the gifts listed in Romans 12 (prophesying, serving, teaching, encouraging, contributing to the needy, leading) describe a church body where everybody had only

> If the whole body were an eye, where would the sense of hearing be? If the whole body were an ear, where would the sense of smell be?
> —1 Corinthians 12:17

this one gift. As the laughter dies down, begin confessing to one another how you might want the whole church to be just like you.

Meditate on Romans 12:9–21

In the rest of the chapter, Paul heaps one practical application on another—listing more than twenty realistic ways of living as a loving living sacrifice. While it is essentially a list of do's and don'ts, these practical instructions are all rooted in one motive—love. Ponder these four questions: 1) Which of these practical applications of a loving life do you do best now? (You might choose to pick someone else in your group to say this about.) 2) Which one do you struggle most to live up to? 3) Which of these instructions is your church best at? 4) Which one does your church need more help developing?

Privately think about someone who "did you dirty." Paul calls us to refuse to take vengeance but to leave room for God to get even with those who hurt us. Discuss the quote by Valerius Maximus, a Roman author from

> The divine wrath is slow indeed in vengeance, but it makes up for its tardiness by the severity of the punishment.
>
> —Valerius Maximus

the time of Paul. Ponder these questions: If we act in revenge, does God let that be the only punishment they get? To what extent are we stealing God's role when we try to get revenge? How might this apply differently to individuals then to governments or nations? What does it mean to "heap burning coals" on the head of the evildoer by treating them kindly?

CONTEMPLATION ✝ REFLECT AND YIELD

Open a circle of sharing for members of your study by asking: What has God said to you today through His Word?   Next ask, What has God said to *us* today?

PRAYER ✝ RESPOND TO GOD

Set aside a period of totally silent, listening prayer—asking these two questions of God: "What must I do?" and "What must *we* do as a church?"

INCARNATION ✝ LIVE THE WORD

What single thing will I do this week to start changing toward what God wants in my life? Am I willing for this group to check up on me next week?

THE DEBT I OWE

Listening for God through Romans 13:1–14

SUMMARY

C hristians never get out of debt. We are deeply indebted to
God for everything, even though we can never pay Him
back. But we feel indebted to Him anyway.

There are other outstanding debts, too. In Romans 13 Paul
reminds us of what we owe to others. These, too, we can never
pay off. As citizens in a secular nation, we still owe honor to
those in authority over us, for government was established by
God. We owe our government leaders—even evil ones—our
taxes and our submission. Paul said all this to Christians living in
Rome—where the emperor sometimes tortured and executed the
very Christians who were supposed to submit.

But it isn't just powerful governments we owe. We owe each other love. While Paul encourages us to pay off our financial debts, he reminds us we should never stop payment on our debt of love. When it comes to payments on our debt of love, we all have a perpetual payment plan.

SILENCE ✝ LISTEN FOR GOD

Leave your eyes open as you look around listening for God to prompt a sense of debt to others in or outside of the room. Listen. *Shhh.*

PREPARATION ✝ FOCUS YOUR THOUGHTS

What good things does God bring us through other people? (And now a harder question.) What good things does God bring us through governments and government leaders?

READING ✝ HEAR THE WORD

At the time Paul wrote Romans, the persecution of Christians had not reached its peak. In fact, in some cases fleeing to the protection of Rome was a good strategy for Christians. So one might argue that the *very* first Christians may have read Paul's instructions on civil obedience as sensible. However, before long the Roman oppression fell on the Christians with fury (including Paul himself), and they read this passage differently then for sure.

It would have been convenient for them to say "that was then, this is now" and resist Rome, even attempting to overthrow it or assassinate the Emperor. But they did not. Under persecution Christians took the passage just as they had under a more benign government—they submitted and paid their taxes.

While many Christians today face a more benign (even friendly at times) government, it is actually more helpful to see the heroism of the more radical acceptance of this teaching by Christians hiding in the catacombs or waiting to be sent to the lions.

To capture the spirit of the original readers, plan ahead for this reading. Go somewhere catacomb-like, where you can pretend you're hiding from Roman persecution—a cellar, a boiler room, a large closet, a yard barn. Play the role with whispered talking. You might chuckle as you do this, but eventually all will get the idea. With a single candle, gather around as one person reads this letter from Paul on submission. Stop, and let it sink in as the physical context makes the writing take on new meaning.

MEDITATION ✝ ENGAGE THE WORD

Meditate on Romans 13:1–7

List the ways submitting to the governing authorities might become practical to the Roman readers of this book. What are the ways Christians submit today to governing authorities?

In what ways does God establish all such authorities? Was God in control even of getting the infamous Christian-killer Nero into power? Why is this notion important to Paul's coming arguments?

Paul argues that rebelling against government authority is tantamount to rebelling against the God who established it. John Wesley used this argument to persuade Americans their rebellion against the Christian nation of England was wrong. Pretend you were a Methodist in those days—what might your class discussion have been like?

Paul claims that the government authority is God's servant. List the ways government can serve God in accomplishing God's will on earth.

There is no distinction between a Christian authority and a secular one—both can be considered serving God's purposes. Think of ways non-Christians have furthered God's will on earth—especially in your own life.

Paul gives a practical reason to submit to government (fear of punishment), but he also gives a moral reason (conscience). Meditate on these two motivations for doing things like paying taxes or submitting to government. How different is the outcome and attitude in each case?

Think about the quote by *Gone with the Wind* writer Margaret Mitchell on taxes. Connect convenience and benefits in the area of having children. Can you see any similar connection for taxes?

> Death and taxes and childbirth. There's never any convenient time for any of them.
> —Margaret Mitchell

Paying taxes can be coerced, thus we never quite know if we are doing it for conscience's sake or because we have to. But we cannot be forced (at least in free countries) to give respect or honor. Yet Paul says we also owe this to our governing leaders. What does this mean? How can we dishonor or be disrespectful of leaders? What debt do we owe leaders in respect or honor, practically speaking? Give specific examples.

Meditate on Romans 13:8–10

Ponder, then share, the similarities you see between paying off a financial debt and paying the continuing debt of love to others.

While some try to drive a wedge between James and Paul on matters of faith and works, there is no doubt they agree on one matter: love is the essence of Christian living. What are some other terms that could have become the central term—and how would the ensuing Christianity have been different from a love-based religion?

Based on the Mother Teresa quote, what are some ordinary ways others have shown genuine love to you? Tell the story.

> Do not think that love, in order to be genuine, has to be extraordinary.
>
> —Mother Teresa

Can a Christian keep the Ten Commandments—that is not breaking any of them? Can a Christian keep the (second) greatest
commandment? How?

Imagine what a church would be like if everyone always and
continually acted in love. Describe it. Is such a church possible
or impossible?

Meditate on Romans 13:11–14

Paul suggests that judgment is nearer now than ever. How does
an expectancy of the end of time as we know it affect how we
live? If we were pretty sure this was our last year, how would we
live differently?

Without getting off on environ-
mental policy, think about the
principle behind Interior Secretary
James G. Watt's comment. In
what ways is this quote true? In
what ways is it untrue? In what

> We don't have to
> protect the environ-
> ment; the Second
> Coming is at hand.
> —James G. Watt

ways do we personally live or not live by this principle?

Paul is often touted as the justification-by-faith-alone apostle, and rightly so. From these Scriptures, however, respond to the phrase that some add to this first idea: therefore it does not matter at all what we do or how we behave. What surprising sins are listed here with orgies and debauchery?

CONTEMPLATION ✝ REFLECT AND YIELD

Ponder quietly what God is calling you to do. Visualize yourself obeying—as if you are watching a video in your mind.

PRAYER ✝ RESPOND TO GOD

Sit in silence listening for God. When you sense what He is saying, speak out what you think you hear—saying only what you hear Him saying, not your own words of response.

INCARNATION ✝ LIVE THE WORD

How will you change your attitude toward government leaders?

How specifically will you increase payments on your debt of love to others? When will you do it? Who will hold you accountable?

JUDGING DISPUTABLE MATTERS

Listening for God through Romans 14:1–23

SUMMARY

S ome things are black and white. Other things are gray. The Bible sometimes gives explicit commands, and with these things there is no question. For instance, the Bible really means we should not commit adultery. But the Bible doesn't address everything. Even in some of its commands (e.g., remembering the Sabbath), it often leaves the *implementation* up to us. This is where convictions come into play.

Christians variously apply the command of Sabbath-honoring. Some insist on observing the *real* Sabbath (Saturday) while others barely observe Sunday at all (other than attending church). But what do we do in a church with both kinds of people—the strict Christians and the liberated ones? That is the subject of this lesson. The issue in Paul's time was eating meat (virtually all of which had been previously offered to idols), and perhaps keeping the Sabbath and other holy days. There were differences in the Roman church on these disputable matters, so Paul gave his prescription for resolution in chapter 14.

SILENCE ✝ LISTEN FOR GOD

Take three deep breaths, slowly exhale, and let your body relax as you focus on the word *acceptance*.

PREPARATION ✝ FOCUS YOUR THOUGHTS

Go around the circle, and tell how your family observed Sunday when you were a child. Share without judging. Then, name some other family convictions you were raised with—even if your parents were not religious.

Lectio   READING ✟ HEAR THE WORD

The Roman church apparently had two factions regarding behaviors. There was a *conservative group* who wanted to keep some of the old taboos and rules. How could a serious Christian eat meat that in all probability had been offered to idols? There was one God, and not eating meat that had been offered to false gods before being sold by the butcher was a long-standing moral rule for Jews. How could a Christian compromise to eat such meat? Didn't Christians also believe there was only *one* God?

And, what about the Sabbath? Didn't God establish the Sabbath even before the law was given—at creation? Why should Christians ignore the Sabbath?

But there was also a more *liberal group* who considered the old taboos and rules irrelevant to Christian living. They saw no need to avoid eating meat just because some meat had been offered to idols: "So what," they might have said, "I know the idol isn't even real." And they considered the old Sabbath rules a vestige of old Judaism that didn't come over to the Christians who were to worship every day of the week and not consider one day more special than another. With which camp will Paul side?

Read this section by first having someone read the above introduction then a second person answer by reading Paul's reply in Romans 14.

MEDITATION ✝ ENGAGE THE WORD

Meditate on Romans 14:1–8

Outline the logical argument for refusing to eat meat offered to idols. Then outline the other side—the reasons why eating this idol-meat is okay. Do the same for observance of the Sabbath and other special days. Make both the conservative and liberal arguments.

Why is it that Paul considers the person with strong conviction to have weaker faith?

Explain the logic of how Paul uses a slave/master motif to get Roman Christians to quit judging and demeaning others in the church.

Discuss the quote by Olympic athlete Vince Poscente, then connect it with Paul's use of the servant/master metaphor.

> Judgmentalism assumes that you have the right to change someone else. Well, you don't. You only have the right to choose how you will change and behave.
>
> —Vince Poscente

Paul is not addressing *in*disputable matters here, but disputable ones. How does the church sort between absolutes and relative ones that become personal convictions? What matters do we in this group agree are clearly *in*disputable—absolutes? What are the three most pressing disputable matters in your church? How could we summarize Paul's direction here in a bumper-sticker-type, crisp statement?

Meditate on Romans 14:9–18

Paul is not against judgment here, but *who* gets to do the judging. In Paul's scheme of things we all get judged. Who does this judging? Why then is it dangerous for us to do it?

While we cannot know for sure, how do you imagine each Christian would give an account of himself to God? How do you imagine this?

How can liberals cause conservatives to stumble in their walk with God? Could conservatives do this to liberals too? How?

Paul admits his own position on the meat—how does he view the thing itself: good or bad? What is the primary factor for Paul making a disputable matter either good or bad?

This chapter begins with a mind-your-own-business call, then moves to a mind-your-brother's-business call. Find the phrases and words that are evidence of this shift, and discuss them.

There can be debate over idol-meat and Sabbath breaking, but there is no debate that destroying your brother or no longer acting in love is wrong. Give examples of how both liberals and conservatives in your church can act in love on current disputable matters.

Ponder Jesus' quote from the Sermon on the Mount. How does being judgmental of others when we "dish it out" come back and bite us later? When? From whom?

Do not judge, or you too will be judged. For in the same way you judge others, you will be judged.

—Jesus of Nazareth (Matthew 7:1-2)

Talk about the Herbert Samual quote on how we tend to feel more virtuous when we can find and condemn apparent vices in others. Is a judgmental attitude inversely related to true personal virtue?

> The virtue of some people consists wholly in condemning the vices in others.
>
> —Herbert Samual

Meditate on Romans 14:19–23

Think up examples of words and actions that lead to *peace* and *mutual edification* in the church when people disagree.

Paul brings the chapter to a mighty conclusion in the final verse by bringing faith into the equation—"everything that does not come from faith is sin." While this appears to be relativism, we must remember this chapter addresses disputable matters. Explain how, in this area of disputable matters, one person can do something with a free conscience while another couldn't do it or it would be sin. Give examples.

CONTEMPLATION ✝ REFLECT AND YIELD

What is it I can do to change my attitude toward other people with whom I might disagree on disputable matters? In what way do I need to change my actions toward them?

PRAYER ✝ RESPOND TO GOD

Silently kneel in prayer, listening for God to bring to your heart people you might tend to be judgmental of or look down on.

INCARNATION ✝ LIVE THE WORD

For the people you've tended to judge, what can you say to them to improve things? When will you say it? Who will hold you accountable to be sure you really do this?

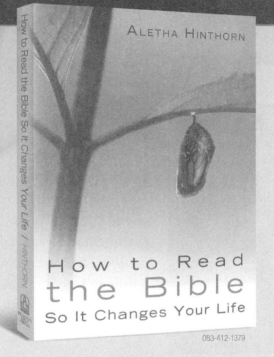

Romans

A Commentary for Bible Students

Clarence L. Bence

An excellent resource for personal study, especially helpful for those involved in the teaching ministries of the church. Wesleyan Bible commentaries will encourage and promote life change in believers by applying God's authoritative truth in relevant and practical ways.

0-89827-157-6
Hardback

$15.99
248 pages

CLARENCE L. BENCE, PH.D., is a professor of church history and theology at Indiana Wesleyan University in Marion, Indiana. He is an ordained minister in The Wesleyan Church, a former pastor and administrator, and speaks extensively at camps, retreats and college campuses.

For additional volumes of The Wesleyan Bible Commentary series visit
www.wesleyan.org/wph.

Order today from your local Christian bookstore!